DATE DUE

		PRINTED IN U.S.A.

D0516198

EVLD WITHDRAWN

Gypsum Public Library
P.O. Box 979 / 47 Lundgren Blvd.
Gypsum, CO 81637
(970) 524-5080

Comments from the Instagram account @hotdudesreading

"I have been following this account for so long and it's the only good decision I've ever made."
—*@kathreens*

"The account owner needs to chill but like in 20 years, not yet; because I enjoy the captions."
—*@katfang*

"This IG is gold and a gift from Jesus."
—*@s_veazie*

"You make my day so often. Thank you. You'll get a man soon enough."
—*@tpwills*

"I feel like hot dudes are reading in public because of this Insta page."
—*@jshulde*

"Following you might be the best decision I've ever made."
—*@ohmeavocadohmy*

"Came for the hot dudes, stayed for the captions."
—*@mflana*

"Marry me. I'll cook and clean."
—*@theupwardfacingdog*

"Caption game is very much fleeking."
—*@natexoh*

"This acct is y I wake up in the morning."
—*@jackiecrespo*

"BRILLIANT AND FKG HILARIOUS."
—*@trippidy*

"I thought only Disney created things this beautiful."
—*@sylmamaaaa*

"This account is a true gift to humanity."
—*@skowronskus*

"Seriously. These captions though! Sheer brilliance!"
—*@amenaravat*

"Who runs this. I want to marry you."
—*@kristenannelies*

"God bless the amount of thought you put into your captions. Beautiful. You're beautiful."
—*@cassieperalta*

Hot
Dudes
Reading

ATRIA BOOKS

New York   London   Toronto   Sydney   New Delhi

ATRIA BOOKS

An Imprint of Simon & Schuster, Inc.
1230 Avenue of the Americas
New York, NY 10020

Copyright © 2016 by Next Thursday?! LLC

All rights reserved, including the right to reproduce this book or portions thereof in any form whatsoever. For information, address Atria Books Subsidiary Rights Department, 1230 Avenue of the Americas, New York, NY 10020.

First Atria Books hardcover edition April 2016

ATRIA BOOKS and colophon are trademarks of Simon & Schuster, Inc.

For information about special discounts for bulk purchases, please contact Simon & Schuster Special Sales at 1-866-506-1949 or business@simonandschuster.com.

The Simon & Schuster Speakers Bureau can bring authors to your live event. For more information, or to book an event, contact the Simon & Schuster Speakers Bureau at 1-866-248-3049 or visit our website at www.simonspeakers.com.

Interior design by Julian Peploe

Manufactured in the United States of America

10 9 8 7 6 5 4 3 2 1

Library of Congress Cataloging-in-Publication Data

Title: Hot dudes reading.
Description: First Atria Books hardcover edition. | New York : Atria Books, 2016.
Identifiers: LCCN 2015049947 (print) | LCCN 2015050982 (ebook) | ISBN 9781501127533 (hardback) | ISBN 9781501127540 (Ebook)
Subjects: LCSH: Men—Humor. | Books and reading—Humor. | BISAC: HUMOR / Topic / Adult. | HUMOR / General.
Classification: LCC PN6231.M45 H68 2016 (print) | LCC PN6231.M45 (ebook) | DDC 818/.5402—dc23
LC record available at http://lccn.loc.gov/2015049947

ISBN 978-1-5011-2753-3
ISBN 978-1-5011-2754-0 (ebook)

To my Instagram followers, who made this book possible: my friends and I love reading your comments and drooling over your submissions, and we sincerely appreciate your support.

To all the beautiful men out there who have been featured on the account: you've all been amazing sports.

And, of course, to the men who are tucked between these covers: I wish I could thank every last one of you between mine. (Seriously. Call me.)

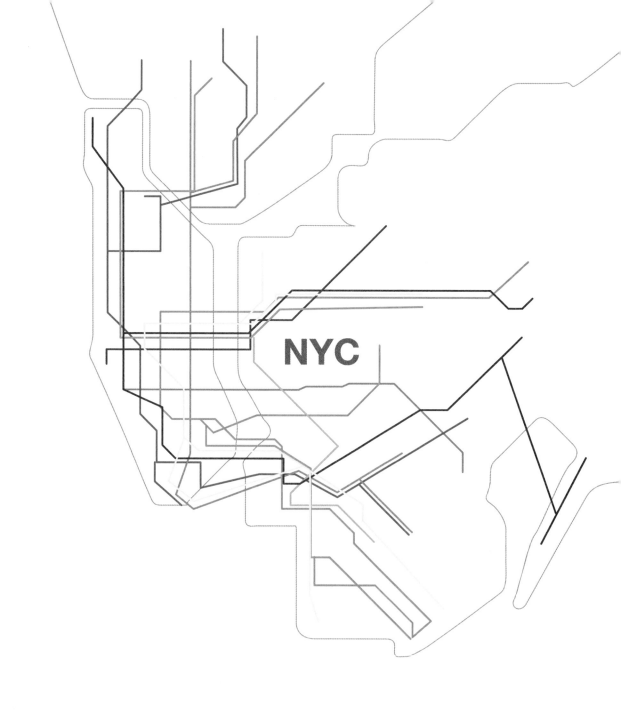

Introduction

Introduction

This is a book about hot dudes reading books. Don't worry, you can thank us later.

The inspiration for this could only come from one place: New York City, Concrete Jungle Where Dreams Are Made. I never expected that my own admittedly inappropriate daydreams about strangers on the subway would find a following on Instagram and lead to writing a book with my best friends, but here we are.

Our story starts with New York City itself. As a young, single resident of this city, you spend a lot of time thinking about your future, everything you want in life, and who you want along for the ride. The energy of this place is contagious, and, as you try to carve out your place amid the chaos, it instills a hunger in you that truly never sleeps.

This is not to say that obsessing over the future is unique to this city, but New Yorkers often find themselves doing it in public. On a weekday, it could be while you're waiting on the subway platform as the F train inexplicably flies past you when you're already ten minutes late for work and nursing a low-grade hangover. On weekends, it could be while you're standing on the sidewalk outside of your favorite brunch spot as you press your face against the window, longing for a table and a Bloody Mary (and maybe some food). During the summer, it could be while you're in an overcrowded train for hours on the way to the beach, or in Central Park looking for respite from the concrete, glass, and steel.

When you're stuck underground with no Wi-Fi, or aboveground

with no eggs Benedict, your mind is free to wander…and for me and my friends, our favorite thing is fantasizing about the men whose paths we cross in our daily lives. As true millennials (mostly), we shared these fantasies with each other over group text. We unanimously agreed that guys reading a good old-fashioned book were more attractive than those swiping away on a smartphone, or the ones just along for the ride, drowning out the world with their headphones.

Then, one hungover morning in February 2015, we decided to share the subjects of our dirtiest daydreams with the world on Instagram. Ever since then, we've connected with hundreds of thousands of people around the world who share our enthusiasm for highly literate hotties. This book is our way of thanking those early supporters, and giving them something they can take home to spend the night with.

This book is also a journey through the city that made all this possible, and brought us all together. We've toured our beloved town along every subway line, from the A/C/E to the J/Z, in search of the hottest book lovers we could find. We also took some detours to interview a few of the guys who originally appeared on our Instagram account so we could find out the truth behind the fictions we created for them.

As you go on this journey with us, we think you'll agree: no matter the season, subway line, or neighborhood, there's a hot dude reading, ready to become the subject of your next great fantasy. Just remember, Jay & Alicia were right: there's literally no one—I mean, nothing—you can't do.

A/C/E

I'm not one to pick favorites, but in the warmer months I go out of my way to ride the A/C/E in the summer swelter. You can find a shirtless stud at Rockaway Beach, a shirtless runner on the West Side Highway, or a shirtless hunk relaxing in Central Park. Okay, so maybe I have a type. #YouDontKnowMe

● **Washington Heights–168th Street**

Whoa! The last time I saw this many muscles, they were bathed in white wine and butter. These may be a different kind, but he looks equally delicious and I'm working up an appetite. Maybe I can convince him to take me out for a nice dinner in the city. "One dozen oysters, please"— hope he gets that hint. #ShuckMe

I keep spotting glimpses of this mysterious man, but Professor Plum and Ms. Peacock over here are getting in my way. Looks like I'll need to move closer to get a clue about the type of guy he really is. Bet we can have a killer time getting to know each other.

#InTheConservatory #WithHisPipe

● Central Park

I was so taken by this beautifully built structure, I almost didn't notice those buildings behind him. I wasted my entire lunch break doing burpees and stretches, hoping he would notice me. Whatever book he's reading had better be good, because these grass stains are going to be hard to explain. #ThereGoesThatPromotion

Times Square—42nd Street

The only reason I'd ever go to Times Square is to catch a Broadway show, but this bag-toting bookworm is a close second. He already has me doing high kicks, so let's hope this Hedwig has more than an angry inch.

#MakeMeHitThoseHighNotes

● 23rd Street

The meticulously dressed Midtown men of the Eighth Avenue line never disappoint, and he's certainly no exception. As well as that jacket fits his broad shoulders, I can't help but think how it would warm me up on a chilly night. I wonder if the same strategy would work if I told him my legs were cold too. #NoJacketNoPantsNoProblem

● The High Line

Hallelujah! If I didn't know any better, I'd say the big guy upstairs was shining a spotlight on this heavenly being. He looks angelic while winding down after a long day of work. Let's hope that halo of his fades when the sun sets, otherwise I'll never get to find out how much better he looks when it rises. #WontBeTheOnlyThingRising

● West 4th Street–Washington Square

Extra, extra! Read all about it: "Hot Men Invading NYC Subway System." That's one headline I wouldn't mind seeing more often, especially if this dashing dude is on the front page. My journalism degree is about to come in handy, because I'm going to do some investigative work for a follow-up piece that would make Woodward and Bernstein proud. #AndDeepThroatToo #ThingsILearnedInCollege

○ Canal Street

Considering his choice of reading material, I can tell this adorable analyst has a head for business and a mind for fun. The fact that he's reading *Freakonomics* must mean he's curious about the hidden side of things, and he's not the only one. I'd like to do my own hands-on research to find out if his lean isn't the only thing that falls to the left.

#LetsSeeThatDemandCurve #AndTheInflationRate

● World Trade Center

This station has me wondering if I've been transported from the subway to the Starship *Enterprise*, because this perfect specimen is out of this world. If there's a planet where flawless creatures like this roam free, then fire up the engines—I'm ready to blast off. #StageFiveKlingOn

● Brooklyn Bridge Park

I was soakin' up some rays on the waterfront when I caught a glimpse of this scruffy stud. Judging by that Hawaiian shirt and his taste in scenic reading spots, I'll bet he's the kind of guy who's into traveling to far-off places. I'm thinking honeymoon suites, Mai Tais on the beach, and couples massages at sunset. Oh screw it . . . #JustLeiMe

● **High Street**

Did I just step onto the A train, or did I wake up as the lovesick star of a John Hughes movie? There hasn't been a boy this crush-worthy in flannel since Jake Ryan made all our birthday wishes come true. This subway isn't exactly a red Porsche, but I'd still let him take me out for a Day Off at our own private Breakfast Club. #ReservationForBabeFroman #SausageKingOfNewYork

◯ **Broadway Junction**

One glimpse of this tan and glowing gent and my

day is already feeling brighter. I'll bet it's hard for him

to readjust to city life after spending time basking in

the sun. As the self-appointed chair of his welcoming

committee, I'm going to try to make his adjustment as

easy as possible so he won't want to leave again.

#DontMindTheHandcuffs

Rockaway Beach

Just rolled over to bronze my back and noticed
this buff beefcake with a good book in hand.
It is definitely *not* T-shirt time over here. He's
a hotter version of the Situation, except with
more brains and none of the baggage. Make
some room on that towel, bro, and I'll teach
you a little something about my own version
of GTL. #Gym #Tan #Lovemaking

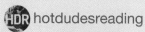

♥ 55,544 likes   💬 5,489

hotdudesreading My heart is anything but still after a glance at this stoic specimen. He's the epitome of perfection, a cross between Michelangelo's *David* and a real-life Ken doll. That's one inanimate object I'd like to bring to life, as long as a certain region doesn't resemble either one of theirs. #WasThereAMarbleShortage? #WhySoSmoothKen? #hotdudesreading

Between the Covers:

An Interview with Ben K., aka "Stoic Specimen"

Hot Dudes Reading: What book were you reading when featured on the account?

Ben K.: I was reading Stephen King's *The Stand*.

HDR: What do you do for a living?

BK: At the moment, I'm modeling for a living.

HDR: Everyone starts somewhere . . . what was your favorite childhood book and why?

BK: I remember thoroughly enjoying *Corduroy*. I believe that was the first book I read. I also have fond memories of reading *Goodnight Opus* with my sisters before bed. Those illustrations will stay with me forever.

HDR: What's your favorite book or author and why?

BK: My favorite author is Fyodor Dostoyevsky. So much so that I've named all of my pets after him.

HDR: You're an old-school guy (so hot)—what makes you choose print books over Kindles or other digital platforms?

BK: I have yet to attempt reading a book on a Kindle. To be completely honest, I'm afraid of them. I'm afraid I'll fall in love with the convenience and won't have the willpower to put it down. I have friends who've gotten hooked and ended up in back alleys doing unmentionable, blow-jobby things for ebooks. I don't want to go down that road if I can help it.

HDR: What's the sexiest thing a girl/guy could be reading?

BK: Anything that shows she's an intellectual. Like Dav Pilkey or Margaret Wise Brown.

HDR: Hardcover or soft-cover?

BK: I prefer soft-cover books.

HDR: Describe to us what it was like when you first saw you had been featured on @hotdudesreading. Go.

BK: It was all thoroughly exciting. The post was brought to my attention by a friend who tagged me in the comments, and I couldn't believe it.

HDR: How has being featured changed your life?

BK: I like to think I'm still the same me. When I was hanging up the posters of it on my wall, I remember telling myself that I wouldn't let this Instagram post go to my head. I've seen *Behind the Music*. I know what groupies can do to relationships. As soon as they show up, I will politely but sternly tell them I'm not interested.

HDR: Have you gotten any dates out of this whole thing? Any long-term relationships? I mean . . . are you single? Will you date me?

BK: I am single, but I haven't procured any dates from the post. I did receive a direct message from a man asking if I was interested in working as an escort. But I don't know if I would really call that stuff "dating."

HDR: Similarly, how many times have you used your appearance on @hotdudes reading to pick up girls/guys?

BK: There was one time when I tried to salvage a derailing date by showing the post as proof that I am contributing to society. Nine months later, that lovely lady gave birth to a beautiful baby boy. With another man, but who's counting?

HDR: Be honest: Have you gotten laid because of this?

BK: Sadly, no. Although, one morning after a night of heavy drinking, I woke up naked in an abandoned train car surrounded by a circle of still-burning candles and an inverted pentagram painted on my chest in pig's blood. So, maybe?

HDR: As a follow-up question, can you then confirm we're doing God's work?

BK: Oh yes, definitely yes.

L

The L train may rank near the bottom in weekend reliability, but when it comes to spotting hot dudes, it's consistently on top. I don't even mind hearing the words "The L train is down," because once I'm out in Brooklyn, I know I'll be getting down too. #BoundForBEDford

Get a ride
in minutes

Download & go.

App Store   Google play

● Montrose Avenue

Holy bulging arms—this is exactly the sort of man I want by my side. I'll bet this huggable Bushwick beast is the type to step up and defend his loved ones in dicey situations, and maybe even turn green in the process. Bad guys wouldn't stand a chance around him, just like his shirt doesn't stand a chance around me. #TheIncredibleHunk

○ Graham Avenue

This Kerouac fan's all-black outfit and long locks are putting a modern twist on the classic Beat Generation vibe. He probably writes his own poetry and can recite entire works by Ginsberg upon request. Hey there, Daddy-O, if you ever get stuck, I can help you finish. #IKnowHowToMakeAManHOWL

● McCarren Park

This beautiful fall weather has me jonesin' for a trip outside the city, so it's a good thing this plaid prince is already dressed for a pumpkin-picking adventure. I hope he doesn't mind getting those perfectly white kicks a little dirty, because I'm planning a detour in the haystacks. #OneHelluvaHayride

● East River State Park

I stopped dead in my tracks when I spotted this blue-hued beauty on my morning run. He's so engrossed in that book, I'll bet he doesn't realize I've been pretending to tie my shoelaces for the last five minutes. Hopefully he'll look up and enjoy his view as much as I'm enjoying mine. #LoopSwoopAndPullMeIn

● St. Mark's Place

My caffeine addiction won't be the only thing bringing me to the coffee shop if this piping hottie is waiting out front with a strong cup of joe. People always say they like their men the same way as their coffee, and I have to agree: first thing in the morning.
#AndAgainInTheAfternoon
#OnceMoreAfterDinner

● Third Avenue

All dressed up on the L? This enticing entrepreneur must have a big pitch today. He's so adorable that I'd buy whatever he's selling. Orange-scented toilet paper? Have to have it. Battery-powered scissors? Completely reasonable! The purrfect cat tower? I'll take two! #IDontEvenHaveACat

● 14th Street–Union Square

Lucky for me, I caught this stylish suitor right as he was settling in for a long commute home. From the looks of his crisp jacket and those wild socks, he's clearly not afraid to show off a few of his favorite colors. In fact, he's done such a good job that I feel like I should show him mine.

#NudeGoesWithEverything

○ **Eighth Avenue**

Is there any better way to end my tour of the city's most attractive subway line than here in the Meatpacking District? I'm tempted to ask this delicious dude for a live demo on how the neighborhood got its name, but I should probably take a hint from that sign behind him and take it easy. Besides, if he makes the first move, that's exactly what I'll be.

#LikeTakingCandyFromABaby

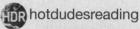

♥ 31,842 likes 💬 1,506

hotdudesreading This Brooklyn-bound babe is rocking some serious artistic style. He's either on his way to referee a Kan Jam tournament in McCarren Park (that's a thing, right?) or coming back from a *Beetlejuice 3* audition. I hope it's the latter because I'm sure he'd have no problem making me call out his name three times. #TakeMeToYourNetherWorld #hotdudesreading

Between the Covers:
An Interview with Ramzy M., aka "Beetlejuice"

Hot Dudes Reading: What book were you reading when featured on the account?

Ramzy M.: Dave Eggers's *A Hologram for the King.*

HDR: What do you do for a living?

RM: I'm a senior designer at Nickelodeon.

HDR: Everyone starts somewhere . . . what was your favorite childhood book and why?

RM: Haha, it's a book called *Anansi the Spider.* It's a kid's book based on the Ashanti tale of how the moon came to find its place in the sky. The illustrations are really gorgeous.

HDR: What's your favorite book or author and why?

RM: Dave Eggers. I've always been a fan; recently I read *The Circle* and couldn't get enough. It raises so many important questions about privacy in the information age.

HDR: You're an old-school guy (so hot)—what makes you choose print books over Kindles or other digital platforms?

RM: We spend enough time staring at a glowing screen. I appreciate the tactile sensation of thumbing through dog-eared pages. That, and when I'm finished they're like trophies—like taxidermied animals to a game hunter.

HDR: What's the sexiest thing a girl/guy could be reading?

RM: Haha . . . this is such a complicated question. I think Bukowski is sexy. Any of the Beat poets and writers. Camus, Nietzsche, Animorphs, Goosebumps. Shel Silverstein.

HDR: Hardcover or soft-cover?

RM: Soft-cover is easier to hold and read on the go. Hardcover looks better on a shelf, though! Books are meant to be used, so I'm in the soft camp. Such an unsexy answer, I know.

HDR: Describe to us what it was like when you first saw you had been featured on @hotdudesreading. Go.

RM: A childhood friend of mine texted me a screenshot. I was honestly pretty surprised—I know I'm no dog, but compared to the other men on the feed I felt like the black sheep. I'm honored and flattered no less! And the caption has provided my friend group with endless laughs. Whoever writes these things needs their own TV show. Or a book. Oh, wait.

HDR: How has being featured changed your life?

RM: Not much, really. I've had a couple dates pull it up and ask me if that's me. I think my ex-boyfriends have seen it (which is endlessly satisfying). My mom is, like, super proud.

HDR: Have you gotten any dates out of this whole thing? Any long-term relation-ships? I mean . . . are you single? Will you date me?

RM: Haha, I can't say I've brought it up of my own volition. Seems tacky, no? *Hey, look, I was on this Instagram so you should date me!* I am currently single, so yes, call me?

HDR: Similarly, how many times have you used your appearance on @hotdudes-reading to pick up girls/guys?

RM: Never.

HDR: Be honest: Have you gotten laid because of this?

RM: I don't know if I can say there was a direct correlation, but I have had sex with people who saw the post and thought it was funny.

HDR: As a follow-up question, can you then confirm we're doing God's work?

RM: *Gloria in excelsis deo. Et in terra pax hominibus.* Amen.

1/2/3

Caution—you are now entering the red zone. These lines can be dangerous to ride, with too many hot dudes to count. You can collide with a gorgeous grad on his way to class or find yourself in a staring contest with a Bowling Green bookworm. Once you find a mate, the rest is as easy as 1-2-3. **#JustLikeMe #JK #Kinda**

Columbia University

Starting my day up on campus, and class is definitely in session. It's always a welcome bonus spotting a dude who has the brawn to match the brains, and this hot T.A. has plenty to spare. I might have to swing by his office hours to show him what T&A really stands for. **#HandsOnLearning**

○ **72nd Street**

Judging by the tattered pages and taped-up binding, this

is a guy who knows what he likes and keeps going back

for more. He's definitely a regular at all the neighborhood

spots. It's only a matter of time before his waiter knows

my order, his bartender pours my usual, and his doorman

waves me right in every night. **#AndOutEveryMorning**

● Columbus Circle

When it comes to The Five Love Languages, I've always wondered which one I speak. I'll bet this brainy blond is fluent in all of them, so maybe he can play interpreter and help me figure it out. Full disclosure—I've never been that great with foreign tongues. #ButHisWillDoJustFine

● 34th Street–Penn Station

I can't say I've ever enjoyed being in Penn Station, but this classic cutie is making this sweatbox tolerable. It's always refreshing to see a guy confident enough to rock a plain white tee. Add him to the list alongside Marlon Brando, James Dean, and Adam Levine . . . but there's another list I'd like to add him to first.

#AnotherNotch #ThisBeltIsGettingTight

● Christopher Street Pier

Is this guy serious? With that grade-A beard, the perfect man bun, and a top-notch reading spot, this dreamy trifecta of man-meat looks too good to be true. If he didn't look so comfortable on that bench, I'd cozy right up next to him and show him he's not the only one who prefers it horizontal. #AndVertical #AndDiagonal #WHATDoesThatEvenMean

Pier 40

This sexy striker must be killing time before his next

scrimmage, and I'd love to be picked first to help

warm him up. Normally I try to stay away from sports

where balls go flying at my nose, but for him I'll make

an exception. Here's to hoping I can handle his drills.

#ThereGoesMySocialLife

● Houston Street

Perfect timing—we're nearing the end of the line just as he's coming to the end of his book. I should swoop in and suggest we discuss it over drinks, even though I haven't exactly read it yet. Not a problem: I've had to fake my way through more important conversations before. #Only5to7DrinksAWeekDoc #ISwear

○ **Bowling Green**

This hypnotizing hipster is a welcome change of pace among the usual FiDi suits, especially with that tattoo peeking out from under his shirt. I wonder what other surprises he has hiding up his sleeve. **#OrDownHisPants**

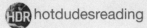

♥ 44,570 likes   💬 5,558

hotdudesreading Forget about #manbunmonday—I could see myself settling into a routine with this hunk every other day of the week and twice on Sundays. He looks like the tough but sensitive CrossFit trainer with a permanently sold-out class that everyone is dying to get into. But those fitness groupies will never get to see him the way I will—hair down, soaking those muscles in the tub with a good book surrounded by candles and bubbles. #UpCloseAndPersonalTraining #hotdudesreading

Between the Covers:

An Interview with Ben R., aka "Man Bun"

Hot Dudes Reading: What book were you reading when you were featured on the account?

Ben R.: I was reading *Dream of the Red Chamber*.

HDR: What do you do for a living?

BR: I'm currently an account executive on the BrightEdge new business team.

HDR: Everyone starts somewhere . . . what was your favorite childhood book and why?

BR: This is super cliché, but *Harry Potter and the Philosopher's Stone*. Certainly pays to have British friends! There was nothing like it; I didn't read it, I devoured it. I still marvel at the complex sentence structure, coupled with the satisfying and approachable language. Reading that book going into a double-digit birthday showed me what was possible when finding the right book at the right time.

HDR: What's your favorite book or author and why?

BR: I read a ton of graphic novels and pepper in contemporary and modern fiction. Guilty pleasures? Addiction memoirs. Favorite authors would be William Styron, Chuck Palahniuk, William Burroughs (I have a hamsa tattoo covering my leg with Burroughs's eye as the centerpiece), Toni Morrison, Charles Bukowski, and many others.

HDR: You're an old-school guy (so hot)—what makes you choose print books over Kindles or other digital platforms?

BR: There's such a satisfying feeling researching a book, going into a local bookshop or specialty shop in the city, making that purchase, and cracking it open at home. While I discover new books through social media, the *New York Times*, the *Wall Street Journal*'s book reviews, etc., seeking books out and holding them in my hands lowers the volume in my digital life. I have an iPad that I read DC Comics on, as well as business and sales books, but anything that's two feet from my face and glows feels like work.

HDR: What's the sexiest thing a girl/guy could be reading?

BR: I'm not the guy for this question. Similar to the old adage, "You can't judge a book by its cover," you can't judge someone's character by their book. "Hey, *Canterbury Tales*! How are you liking it?" "Umm . . . there's just, like, SO much. My professor . . ."

HDR: Hardcover or soft-cover?

BR: Hardcover at home. You can take the time to fold and crease her pages in a uniform way, and boy does she look pretty. I'd say soft-cover for on-the-go because, let's face it, she's up for anything. Shove her in a bag, break her open on a crowded train, roll around in the sand, and dab at the pages when she gets wet. Softcover are stories in motion. What am I saying, soft-cover. Soft-cover for the win.

HDR: Describe to us what it was like when you first saw you had been featured on @hotdudesreading. Go.

BR: LOTS of messages of support from my girlfriend's friends and cheeky texts from people in high school I haven't talked to in years. I was a little ashamed, as I'd just started the book I was photographed with, so being twenty pages deep wasn't the best impression to the Internet horde.

HDR: How has being featured changed your life?

BR: I have two weird metrics in my life right now: Instagram likes surpassing 40,000, and 5,000-plus comments from individuals all over the world. I'm a huge hit in Toledo, Ohio, thanks to my girlfriend's family. Did it make work a little awkward for a little while? And did I love that it made work a little awkward for a while? Yes and yes.

HDR: Have you ever used your appearance on @hotdudesreading to your advantage?

BR: Haven't had the opportunity, though it is a great icebreaker when a friend says I'm really big on Instagram. It's the ultimate wingman tool, especially when they find out I'm unavailable. The girls are intrigued by the HDR guy, but they stay for my available and very charming friend.

HDR: Be honest: Have you gotten any of your friends laid because of this?

BR: Every wingman feels at least a fraction of a percent responsible for getting his buddy in a lady's good graces, so if we added up all those percentages, it may add up to one "lay."

HDR: As a follow-up question, can you then confirm we're doing God's work?

BR: Keep it up! Spread your literary gospel of commuter reading and man-meat to the masses! HDR book clubs with some of your more colorful features? Sign me up as an acolyte and evangelist—I'm a patient and gentle teacher.

4/5/6

The 4/5/6 is the perfect train line to take you to all of the places where you can live out your literary fantasies. Pick up a modern-day Gatsby on the Upper East Side, spot a contemporary Holden Caulfield in Grand Central Terminal, or search for your very own Moby Dick on the next boat leaving South Ferry. And who knows, you may even end up scoring a one-on-one Breakfast at Tiffany's with your dream man. #DontGoLightlyOnMe

● Wall Street

The 6 train may be old and tired, but my late-night ride just got a fresh new look. This Wall Street stud is burning the midnight oil, because money never sleeps . . . and we won't either. #StocksAndBondage

● Brooklyn Bridge—City Hall

Hey stranger, what are you doing all dressed

up in white with nowhere to go? How about

I take you by the hand and march you up

to City Hall to make an honest man of you?

Don't worry, it'll be a quick ceremony, because

I'm already planning ahead for the honeymoon.

#ConsummationStation

● Bleecker Street

On my way to meet a friend for drinks, my jaw literally fell open when I spotted this California dream. Maybe it's his brawny arms, or that tropical print jacket, but he looks like he spends his days surfing and his nights throwing back Longboard Lagers. I'm sure there are a few tricks he could show me, but all I want to know is if he can hang ten. #Inches #ThatsWhatItMeansRight?

◯ 14th Street–Union Square

Maybe not the best place to read a book, but it looks like no one's complaining. He's clearly not afraid to get down in inappropriate places, so we should find another spot to get personal. Where's an empty train car when you need one? #ImTheConductorNow

● 33rd Street

Now this is my kind of 2-for-1 special. No need for happy hour, because I'm already drunk in love with both of these gorgeous gents. How do I decide between Mr. Business in the back or Mr. Party in the front? Maybe I don't have to . . . I've always been told that two's a crowd. #AndThreesAParty

● St. Patrick's Cathedral

The higher powers must be trying to get me
to church if they're planting bait like this on
the front steps. I'd already be owning up to all
the thoughts this angel is putting in my head
if I wasn't worried about needing a marathon
confession session. But then again, the best part
about coming clean is getting a little dirty first.
#SqueezeMePleaseMeThenFebrezeMe

Hot damn. This stud is what all of my high school fantasies were made of: a gorgeous face, prom king hair, and a lacrosse captain's body. I'll bet he was no stranger to "that spot" under the bleachers. Let's just hope he wasn't too busy to take Home Ec, because I'm about to rip off all of those buttons. #LikeItsPromNight

Based on this clean-cut charmer's perfectly pressed suit, I'm thinking he's got it all together. I'm picturing a high-rise apartment with a fully stocked kitchen and color-coded closet. He probably even folds his fitted sheets. I'll be happy as long as his thread count is higher than my bank account. #ThreeFigures

● 161st Street–Yankee Stadium

I was rushing down the stairs late to the game when this big boy made me slam on the brakes—I wasn't expecting to see a jock like him outside the park. Suddenly I stopped caring about the action on the field and could only focus on scoring. He may not be one of the players, but he's definitely getting to third base tonight. #AndWavingHimHome

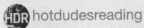

♥ 28,709 likes   💬 1,415

hotdudesreading His book may be in rough shape, but this dude is re-FINE-d. He looks like he's about to step onstage for Shakespeare in the Park, and I'll gladly be his Juliet. Thankfully he can't hear the soliloquy forming in my head. #MontagueMe #hotdudesreading

Between the Covers:

An Interview with Jon J., aka "Romeo"

Hot Dudes Reading: What were you reading when featured on the account?

Jon J.: *Confessions of an Economic Hit Man* by John Perkins.

HDR: What do you do for a living?

JJ: I work for an engineering design and consultancy firm in Midtown. I am a mechanical engineer.

HDR: Everyone starts somewhere . . . what was your favorite childhood book and why?

JJ: *The Alchemist*. Santiago is a curious and courageous young boy in search of "the possible." *The Alchemist* is an exciting and relatable story about pursuing passion and purpose, personal development, and the attainment of a higher consciousness. As a boy, and to this day, I find myself filled with the same sentiments, asking the same questions, and seeking the same ends.

HDR: What's your favorite book or author and why?

JJ: *Rocket Boys* by Homer Hickam Jr. Hickam grew up in a coal mining town in West Virginia in the early '60s. He defied expectations, and what appeared to be insurmountable odds, by becoming a NASA engineer. Homer is the embodiment of determination and steadfast diligence; an example that I've always strived to follow.

HDR: You're an old-school guy (so hot)—what makes you choose print books over Kindles or other digital platforms?

JJ: Sometimes the old ways are best.

HDR: What's the sexiest thing a girl/guy could be reading?

JJ: Mystery, horror, science fiction, psychologically driven books . . . anything that engages higher intellect and imagination. A well-nourished and unbridled imagination keeps matters interesting, possibly dangerous, but, more important, far from boring.

HDR: Hardcover or soft-cover?

JJ: Since we're running with the double entendres . . . I say I take things on a case-by-case basis. It depends on the subject matter, and on the intended duration and frequency of usage.

HDR: Describe to us what it was like when you first saw you had been featured on @hotdudesreading. Go.

JJ: I remember being very confused. I got a few screenshots from several friends in addition to accusations that I had been posing on the E train to promote reading among today's youth.

HDR: How has being featured changed your life?

JJ: Mom keeps urging me to use my newfound "power" to find a girlfriend, settle down, and extend the family.

HDR: Have you gotten any dates out of this whole thing? Any long-term relationships? I mean . . . are you single? Will you date me

JJ: No, actually, and quite single. What time am I picking you up?

HDR: Similarly, how many times have you used your appearance on @hotdudesreading to pick up girls/guys?

JJ: I'd never bring it up; hate to blow my own horn.

HDR: Be honest: Have you gotten laid because of this?

JJ: No, ma'am/sir, but it's still early.

HDR: As a follow-up question, can you then confirm we're doing God's work?

JJ: Absolutely. You're providing wingman services to a handful of deserving gentlemen, promoting extracurricular/leisure reading worldwide, and you're giving girls and young women a new standard for boyfriends to strive for. Well done, HDR. Seriously, though.

B/D/F/M

The B/D/F/M is like a tasting room with a variety of flavors. You can pick up an earthy Lower East Side artist on Essex, or, if you're in the mood for something rich, you can snag a smoky suit at 30 Rock. Either way, you'll be sure to find something that goes down smooth.

#IllTakeASixPack

● 96th Street

This devilishly handsome dude is putting all kinds of naughty ideas in my head. The way he's leaning up against that pole makes me wonder if he's about to give everyone on the train a Magic Mike moment. Good thing I have a front-row seat and enough singles to make it rain in here.

#MeetMeInTheChampagneRoom #JustOneMoreSong

● 72nd Street

I hardly noticed the train has been stuck in the station for the last five minutes because I've been busy staring down this cut-up cutie. Those rips are giving me a good preview of the man underneath, and I'm itching to see more. Good thing he doesn't mind a little wear and tear, because I'm not much of a seamstress. #ButIdStillThreadHisNeedle

● Bryant Park

I nearly choked on my lunch today when I noticed this dude next to me. A near-death experience would be totally worth it if it means he'll come to the rescue with the Heimlich. I've got a few other maneuvers in mind that I'd use to return the favor. #MoreLikeHeimLICK

○ Madison Square Park

I'm usually drooling over a different kind of meat at the city's best burger joint, but this man has me wildly distracted. He looks ready to settle in for a nice afternoon in the park, and I hope this piece of grade-A beef wants company. After comparing notes on our favorite authors and a nice stroll through the park, maybe we can share a patty or two.

#WaitTillHeSeesMyBuns

● Broadway–Lafayette Street

This focused fox doesn't seem to even notice the impromptu concert going on over his shoulder. I wonder what it'll take to get his undivided attention. Maybe show off my brass? Diddle his fiddle? Either way, my performance is going to end with a standing O.

#OrTwo

● Delancey Street–Essex Street

Surprise, surprise: another delay on the F train. For once I don't mind, since it gives this guy more time to put down that book and make a move. He'll soon learn that some things are worth the wait—like the next installment of *Game of Thrones*, the latest iPhone, and holding off till marriage. #OrSoTheySay #WhoTheHellAreThey?

○ **Prospect Park**

A big guy and a small fry—swoon! This dreamy

daddy might be taken, but who says I can't look?

He's got it all: the band, the baby, and the bod.

Time for me to take a stroll and find a man of my

own. They don't call it Prospect Park for nothin'.

#GonnaBeALongStroll #BroughtMyWalkingShoes

Church Avenue

No A.C. on this train? That shouldn't be a problem. The steamier the better with this spicy stud. I think we're only about two degrees away from him ripping that tank off or me completely passing out . . . from the heat, I promise.

#StayCool #YouGotThis #MaybeNot #SendHelp

● Kings Highway

I'm not sure if it's the gorgeous gent or the smell of the trash pile behind him that's making me weak in the knees, but that's the risk you take getting on the empty car of a crowded train. As soon as the doors open, I'm getting the hell out of here, and you'd better believe I'm taking him with me. #NoHotDudesLeftBehind

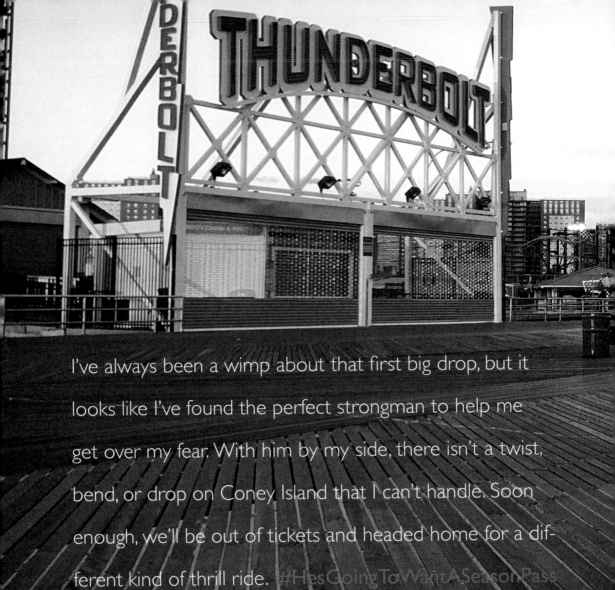

I've always been a wimp about that first big drop, but it looks like I've found the perfect strongman to help me get over my fear. With him by my side, there isn't a twist, bend, or drop on Coney Island that I can't handle. Soon enough, we'll be out of tickets and headed home for a different kind of thrill ride. #HesGoingToWantASeasonPass

Coney Island

♥ 35,691 likes 💬 1,610

hotdudesreading I love a man who makes a statement, and this guy looks like a top model who just finished walking the runway at fashion week. I'm trying hard to contain my inner fangirl, but part of me wants to run up to him like a teenager trying to get an autograph at a One Direction concert. If only I had some-where he could put his signature. Hmm, on second thought . . . #PutYourHancockOnMe #NYFWM #hotdudesreading

Between the Covers:

An Interview with Victor R., aka "New York Fashion Week Model"

Hot Dudes Reading: What book were you reading when featured on the account?

Victor R.: Oddly enough, I was reading *How to Be an Adult: A Handbook on Psychological and Spiritual Integration* by David Richo.

HDR: What do you do for a living?

VR: I am a father to my nine-year-old son, and I get paid to model and act. I'm also a poet and aspiring photographer.

HDR: Everyone starts somewhere . . . what was your favorite childhood book and why?

VR: *There's a Nightmare in My Closet* by Mercer Mayer. The boy opened himself up to his fear, faced his fear, and became friends with it.

HDR: What's your favorite book or author and why?

VR: The book at the moment would be *Illusions: The Adventures of a Reluctant Messiah* by Richard Bach. My favorite author is Kahlil Gibran because I love his style. His work feels like it has the essence of Whitman and the power of the Old Testament.

HDR: You're an old-school guy (so hot)—what makes you choose print books over Kindles or other digital platforms?

VR: Books feel real. I write as well, including poetry, so I respect the process. Digital feels easy. Yes, I completely understand that digital is an art form and has its place as a platform to get content out. I just like to take a break from the screen and feel a page, have a bookmark, and pick up where I left off. I'm on the phone all day with e-mails and phone calls and other mindless activities, so a book feels like a break and an exploration.

HDR: What's the sexiest thing a girl/guy could be reading?

VR: Anything that expands one's consciousness. Your kid's homework, self-help, poetry, essays, spiritual texts, braille, metaphysics, art, *How to (insert subject) for Dummies*, a manual, whatever gets your rocks off. Anything that's a step in the direction of discovering yourself and your likes and wants and figuring out what your purpose is and what you were put on this planet to do.

HDR: Hardcover or soft-cover?

VR: Why does this sound like the most intimate question ever? I would have to say soft, but really, really fat.

HDR: Describe to us what it was like when you first saw you had been featured on @hotdudesreading. Go.

VR: *Why did I not notice the ninja who took the photo? . . . Why are my pants so freaking skinny? . . . Who let me leave the apartment in pants so skinny? . . . Why am I sitting like that? . . . Who is the lady next to me mean-mugging? . . . Why is my man purse just wide open? . . . Why is my hat sitting so far up on my head? . . . I hate shaving.* Just a couple thoughts that popped into my head when I saw the photo. P.S. Whoever wrote the description on my photo, all you had to do was ask for my autograph!

HDR: How has being featured on @hotdudesreading changed your life?

VR: I don't think it has changed my life. Friends thought it was hilarious I got caught and featured. So it has sparked fun conversations. There were a bunch of hilarious comments left on the image. 34,758 likes. That is crazy—I'm just reading on the train.

HDR: Have you gotten any dates out of this whole thing? Any long-term relationships? I mean . . . are you single? Will you date me?

VR: I'm not sure I have gotten a date out of it. Maybe hit on through Instagram. No long-term relationships. I am single. I don't even know if you are a man or woman or a child in Cambodia. All I know is you have access to a computer. You might be in prison? I am fresh out of a break-up, so I am licking my wounds. I'll be back on the market soon.

HDR: Similarly, how many times have you used your appearance on @hotdudesreading to pick up girls/guys?

VR: NEVER. Should I try that?

HDR: Be honest: Have you gotten laid because of this?

VR: Does solo count?

HDR: As a follow-up question, can you then confirm we're doing God's work?

VR: You're doing a good deed. Maybe I'll have this image put on posters and spread them around town and put on T-shirts.

G

The G train may be slow, but once you're on it, it rocks you—just like the men who ride it. It's safe to assume these Brooklyn babes have a healthy dose of patience and know the benefits of waiting their turn. After all, the express train may be fun, but **#IDontWantNoOneMinuteMan**

Court Square

Ooh, la la. Noticed this beautiful beau reading in French (swoon). Other than kissing and toast, the only French I know is, "Voulez-vous coucher avec moi?" Not totally sure what it means, but if it worked for the girls of *Moulin Rouge*, then I'm sure it'll do the trick for me, right? #GiuchieGiuchieYaYaDaDa

● Greenpoint Avenue

Riding the G train through Brooklyn, I knew I would see some serious beards, but this guy has surpassed my expectations. He would look more at home chopping wood at our cabin in the Catskills, right before making us a delicious dinner with fish from the day's catch. #BaitAndTackleMe

Benefits, payroll, and everything you need to take care of your team.

Meet Justworks.

JUSTW

Carbon
EFF

tru

Check out this handsome historian reading

about *Other People's Money*. It just so happens

I'm a specialist in the field and can teach him all

he needs to know over drinks—and then over

dinner, and then over eggs and pancakes in the

morning. #OverEasy #HeButterNotBisQuick

Fulton Street

Something about this guy makes me think he's a real sweetheart, like the kind of guy who wouldn't wake a stranger if they fell asleep on his shoulder. Maybe I should slide over there and . . . nope. That's going too far. Right?

#SolCreepYeahhhh

● Bergen Street

I bet this sleek and stylish Brooklynite knows all the hottest spots from Greenpoint to Gowanus. I should probably pretend I'm lost and ask him where to get off—looks like he knows how to find the right G-stop.

#GetYourMindOutofTheGutter

● Fourth Avenue–9th Street

The way the tracks go off into infinity behind this Follett fan has me feeling a little adventurous. I wonder if he's up for a trip to see the real-life Pillars of the Earth with nothing but me and a Eurail pass. No need to pack a change of clothes, babe— we don't need 'em for what I have in mind. #IHaveEnoughBaggageForUsBoth

♥ 28,594 likes   💬 661

hotdudesreading It's taking all of my inner strength to keep from high-kicking my way over to this sporty stud. But for once I'm going to sit back, picture him trading jerseys after an intense soccer match, and wait for him to make the first pass. If his game is as good as I imagine it to be, we'll be playing for keeps soon enough. #LifeGoooaaalll!!! #hotdudesreading

Between the Covers:

An Interview with Jon G., aka "Soccer Stud"

Hot Dudes Reading: What book were you reading when featured on the account?

Jon G.: *Thinking, Fast and Slow* by Daniel Kahneman.

HDR: What do you do for a living?

JG: I run a company called Peach Rise Athletic (@peachrise), which is an athletic wear company. I also work as a personal trainer at Equinox in Manhattan.

HDR: Everyone starts somewhere . . . what was your favorite childhood book and why?

JG: I used to love *Where the Wild Things Are* by Maurice Sendak because it put me in a completely different world. I love books like that.

HDR: What's your favorite book or author and why?

JG: It honestly changes pretty frequently. To date, *Siddhartha* by Herman Hesse is a classic—and a truly incredible piece of work.

HDR: You're an old-school guy (so hot)—what makes you choose print books over Kindles or other digital platforms?

JG: I cannot succumb to the mainstream when it comes to e-reading. Great concept, just not for me.

HDR: What's the sexiest thing a girl/guy could be reading?

JG: I love it when a girl can talk to me about topics of intellect by further questioning the concepts that many great pieces of work provide. If you are an avid *Fifty Shades of Grey* type of book lover, I'm sorry, I will not put a ring on it.

HDR: Hardcover or soft-cover?

JG: Soft-cover.

HDR: Describe to us what it was like when you first saw you had been featured on @hotdudesreading. Go.

JG: It was really funny. My friend, Sydney, first sent me the screenshot, and then about ten to fifteen more people called me or sent me the photo. The first thing I thought was, *Damn, I wish they could have tagged me and my company in the photo* because it got 17,000 likes in a matter of days.

HDR: How has being featured changed your life?

JG: When it first happened, women would say, "Of course this would happen to you" in a sarcastic tone, so thank you @hotdudesreading for that . . . Other than that, I still get made fun of for reading, but now it's at a whole new level. So thank you @hotdudesreading . . .

HDR: Have you gotten any dates out of this whole thing? Any long-term relationships? I mean . . . are you single? Will you date me?

JG: I have gotten no dates, no long-termers. You can say I'm a mingler. I will date you, although no one knows if you are a guy or girl, so I'm skeptical.

HDR: Similarly, how many times have you used your appearance on @hotdudes-reading to pick up girls/guys?

JG: For the nerdy chicks, it does wonders.

HDR: Be honest: Have you gotten laid because of this?

JG: In my caption you stated I was a soccer player. To answer your question, I now enjoy watching women's soccer.

HDR: As a follow-up question, can you then confirm we're doing God's work?

JG: Yes, may God bless your souls.

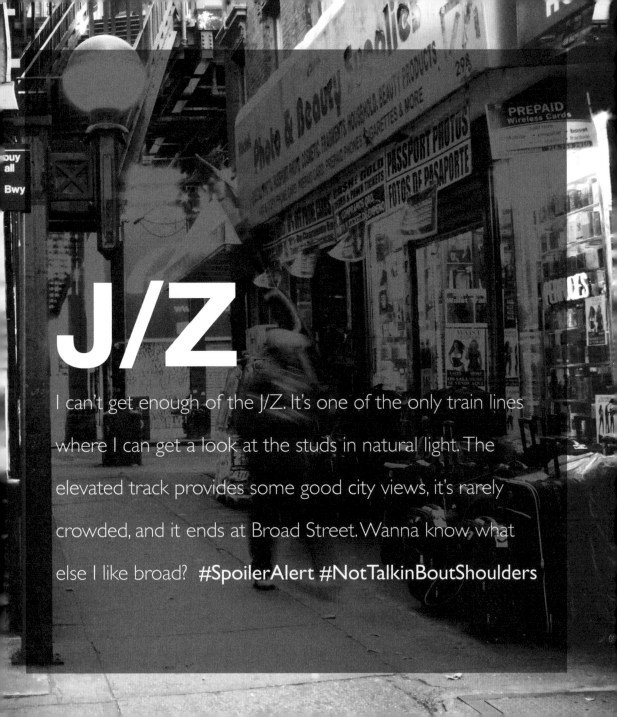

J/Z

I can't get enough of the J/Z. It's one of the only train lines where I can get a look at the studs in natural light. The elevated track provides some good city views, it's rarely crowded, and it ends at Broad Street. Wanna know what else I like broad? #SpoilerAlert #NotTalkinBoutShoulders

● Woodhaven Boulevard

Eric. Caspian. Philip. The Artist Formerly Known As. None of the other princes can hold a candle to this real-life royalty before my eyes. Whatever story he's starring in is one I'll want to read over and over and over again. Only, in this version, I'll take the lead—by grabbing those bars and mounting him like a prince's steed. #ItsMYHappyEnding

○ **Myrtle Avenue**

I've spotted this brooding bachelor on my commute a few times before, but the stained glass is suddenly making me see him in a whole new light. I'm picturing those boots replaced by wingtips, that jacket turning into a tux, and my beaming father walking me down the aisle. Let's just hope no one objects. #WaitNotYou #YoureTheGroom #QuickLockTheDoors

Hewes Street

Exit Broadway & Hooper Street

They say you should be careful walking the streets of NYC alone at night. I feel much better now that I've stumbled upon this chivalrous chaperone enjoying a late-night read. Please take my hand, guide me through the darkness, and make sure I get home safe and sound. #UnlessYourPlaceIsCloser?

● Marcy Avenue

Crossing over the bridge at night always gets me wondering what everyone's lives are like on the other side. Take this buttoned-up babe: he may look all sweet and innocent, but once the buttons come undone, I'll bet he won't be afraid to show off his wild side. Lucky for him, I'll try anything at least once. **#AlreadyGotMySafeWord**

● East River Park

This hunk with a hardcover may be preoccupied with *The New Yorker Stories*, but his favorite New York story is about to happen. It goes like this: future fiancée pretends to trip and fall to get his attention and then accidentally breaks a tooth. #ThoNitheToMeethYou

○ **Bowery**

I'm always on the hunt for my future puppy daddy, and this wholesome hottie reading *The Call of the Wild* has me drooling. While it may not be the best behavior, Rover won't be the only one jumping on him when he walks through our door. With some time and patience, he just might be the one to finally tame me. All I'll need is some positive encouragement and a few tasty treats.

#AndAGoodBoneToo

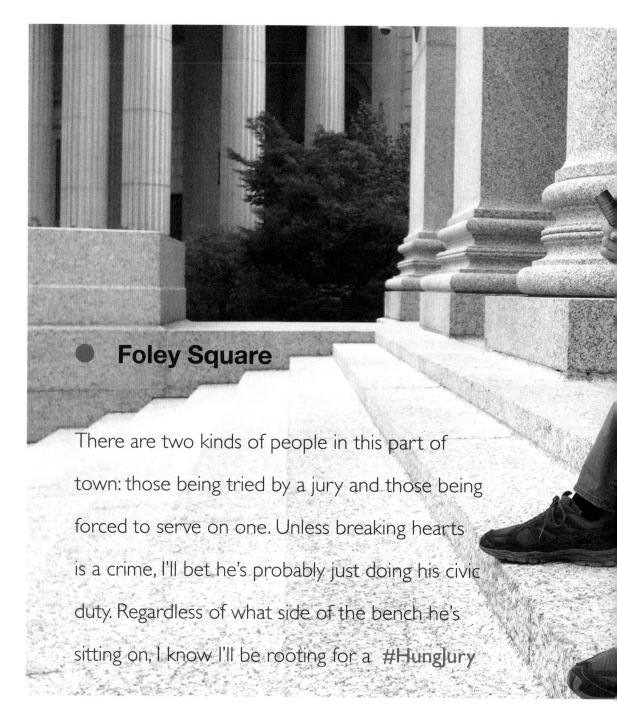

Foley Square

There are two kinds of people in this part of town: those being tried by a jury and those being forced to serve on one. Unless breaking hearts is a crime, I'll bet he's probably just doing his civic duty. Regardless of what side of the bench he's sitting on, I know I'll be rooting for a #HungJury

● **Broad Street**

The coiffed hair and thick glasses make me think this Silicon Valley showstopper has lost his way from the West Coast. I should step in and help him navigate these tricky subways, but he's probably already created an app for that . . . in which case, I'll just focus on getting it in.
#BeforeTheIPO

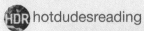

♥ 42,848 likes   💬 1,697

hotdudesreading I mean, honestly, is there anything better than a hot dude reading on the train? How about an art history buff brushing up on the old masters? I really hope he's more into Titian than Pollock, because I'll volunteer as his model. #drawmelikeoneofyourfrenchgirlsjack #hotdudesreading

Between the Covers:
An Interview with John F., aka "History Buff"

Hot Dudes Reading: What book were you reading when featured on the account?

John F.: *Hertzian Tales: Electronic Products, Aesthetic Experience, and Critical Design.*

HDR: What do you do for a living?

JF: Currently, researcher working on creative applications for software and hardware. Some freelance work along those lines as well.

HDR: Everyone starts somewhere . . . what was your favorite childhood book and why?

JF: The Redwall books. Animals in medieval castles with swords and whatnot—they're great.

HDR: What's your favorite book or author and why?

JF: *The Way Things Work* by David Macaulay. My dad used to read it to me. You can spend your whole life reading that book.

HDR: You're an old-school guy (so hot)—what makes you choose print books over Kindles or other digital platforms?

JF: I do digital work all the time. Books are a nice tactile break from that.

HDR: What's the sexiest thing a girl/guy could be reading?

JF: Probably the "Red Hot Reads" section of Cosmo.

HDR: Hardcover or soft-cover?

JF: Soft.

HDR: Describe to us what it was like when you first saw you had been featured on @hotdudesreading. Go.

JF: Confusion, followed by a wave of anxiety. Then I started thinking it was pretty funny as all my friends began to find it.

HDR: How has being featured changed your life?

JF: Now when I read on the subway I'm suspicious of anyone around me who is on their phone.

Central
s Pt & Main St, Qns
on Yards

7

This Queens-bound line is the perfect place to find yourself a king. From the stampede of jocks venturing out to Citi Field (home of the Mets) to the prepsters headed out to the National Tennis Center, it's always easy to score a sporty stud. The train may be a seven,

#ButAllISeeAreTens

● 34th Street–Hudson Yards

Doctor, doctor, ring the alarm. It's a medical emergency, and I'm ready to get on the table for a little bit of special attention. My heart is obviously racing, but I'm pretty sure this will require a more thorough examination.

#OopsThereGoesMyGown

I love it every time I catch a fellow bibliophile leaving the New York Public Library. He'd better get through that book quickly so I can take him back in to check out another one. Hopefully, reading is the only thing he rushes through, because I know exactly what section we're going to first. #GettingSackedInTheStacks #GoingDeepIntoTheCollection

● Grand Central–42nd Street

Cool, calm, and collected amidst the chaos of rush hour?! This balanced babe must spend serious time in the yoga studio to channel that much inner Zen. Warrior, eagle, lotus, my boyfriend—there isn't a position I don't want him in, and I'm not leaving until we try them all. #NamaStayingOver #MakeHimSayOhm

● Vernon Boulevard

I was taking a break from the city in this quaint Queens pub when I noticed a stunner in the smoking (hot) section. I love it when a guy is confident enough to sit alone with just his book and a brew. He looks pretty comfortable in his own world, but maybe if I buy Mr. Independent a few more rounds, he'll start to see things my way. #CoDependencyIsCool #NeedyIsNeat #AttentionIsAwesome

● 82nd Street–Jackson Heights

Just like that sign, my mom always told me courtesy counts. After I'm done thanking the universe for this delicious dude, I'm going to politely ask him to join me for a drink. And later, if he's lucky, I might just throw manners to the wind and invite myself into his bed. #SharingIsCaring #ProbsNotWhatMomMeant

a Manhattan
ck

Late nights take **N** to
36 St, Brooklyn for R

N/Q/R

I've always thought there was something kind of romantic

about riding the vintage cars of the N/Q/R. After all, this is

the line that can take you from the Diamond District for a

little ring shopping, to Central Park for a classic engagement,

and then straight down to City Hall to exchange some vows.

#LimoToTheReception #KeepThatPartitionUp

34   34

DANGER

● Astoria Boulevard

The moment the N train moved above ground I began to see this hard-bodied stud in a new light. Despite his tough exterior, I know that any man reading *The Princess Bride* is a romantic at heart. Here's hoping that when I interrupt him to ask if he's looking for a Princess Buttercup stand-in, he'll respond, "As You Wish." #IDoWish

● 49th Street

Seeking shelter from the mob of tourists above ground, I ducked into the 49th Street subway station to get some space. Once I spotted this dashing dude taking up both seats on that bench, suddenly I had a change of heart. It's not MORE room that I need, it's just A room.

#Hotel #Motel #HolidayInn

⬤ 34th Street

Summer can be brutally hot in the city, but I'm

not complaining if this suited suitor is going to

keep stripping down. I typically love seeing a man

dressed to the nines, but I may have to turn up

the thermostat just to see how far this will go.

#LiteralHotDudeReading

Madison Square Park

I stopped dead in my tracks when I laid eyes on this Robert Pattinson look-alike. I thought vampires couldn't come out during the day, but he sure shines bright in the sun, and I have a feeling he'll be even better in the dark. #ImHereForTheFangBang

○ Prince Street

I'm curious: What exactly constitutes an emergency? Whatever it is, consider me ready to fake one so I can grab this smoke show by the hand, pull him out the exit, and never look back. Just to be safe, I'll rush him straight to the refuge of my apartment till the coast is clear. But he should know, that emergency is the only thing I plan on faking today. #UnlessHeAsksMyAge

Prospect Park

It looks like the grass is actually greener on this dude's side of the path. Hopefully, that's a blanket in his backpack, because I'm so down for a picnic in the park. We can talk about our favorite authors while gazing up at the clouds and sharing wine, cheese, and at least one hard meat.

#HideTheSalami

● Union Street

Spotted this one from across the platform and suddenly decided I should take the scenic route downtown. He looks like the hot, foreign scuba instructor in every cliché romantic comedy, and I'm already imagining him in a more adventurous role. Maybe leading a safari in Africa, or an excursion through the Australian Outback? Hopefully, he'll be right at home when I wrap my arms and legs around him and climb him like a eucalyptus tree.

#KoalaFiedLover

21 train lines, 75 dudes, and 4 boroughs later and I've finally

been caught. But ... I think he's into it. #GameOver

About the Authors

The creators of @hotdudesreading are a group of close-knit friends/marginally functional young professionals in New York City who never dreamed an inside joke about their border-line-inappropriate fantasies about studly bookworms would become an Instagram phenomenon. The account has racked up millions of views and has been covered by the *New York Times, Daily Mail,* BuzzFeed, *Vogue,* and many other fine publications. After almost blowing their entire advance on rosé, they've some-how managed to remain friends (and out of rehab) and can be seen snapping pics and chasing di-, er, dudes all over the city.

Gypsum Public Library
P.O. Box 979/47 Lundgren Blvd.
Gypsum, CO 81637
(970) 524-5080